ROBERTO ATHAYDE was born in Rio de Janeiro, Brazil in 1949. While attending school in Brazil, he was expelled from three separate schools and came to the United States as an exchange student in 1967. He has attended the Sorbonne in Paris and the University of Michigan, each for a single year. His works include the plays: THE RE-ACTIONARY, VISITORS FROM ON HIGH, HANDBOOK FOR SURVIVAL IN THE JUN-GLE, and WAY BACK IN THE FARM. He has been awarded the Molière Prize for play-wrighting excellence and now lives in New York City.

MISS MARGARIDA'S WAY

Tragicomic Monologue for an Impetuous Woman

ROBERTO ATHAYDE

A BARD BOOK/PUBLISHED BY AVON BOOKS

AVON BOOKS
A division of
The Hearst Corporation
959 Eighth Avenue
New York, New York 10019

Copyright © 1977 by Roberto Athayde
Published by arrangement with the author.
Library of Congress Catalog Card Number: 78-74752
ISBN: 0-380-40568-7

First Bard Printing, February, 1979

BARD TRADEMARK REG. U.S. PAT. OFF. AND IN OTHER COUNTRIES, MARCA REGISTRADA, HECHO EN U.S.A.

Printed in the U.S.A.

Miss Margarida's Way, starring Michael Learned, was first presented in the United States at the American Contemporary Theater in San Francisco, opening March 4, 1977. The New York production, starring Estelle Parsons as Miss Margarida and with Colin Garrey as the student, opened August 3, 1977 at the Estelle R. Newman Theatre of the New York Shakespeare Festival, where it played until September 4. The play moved uptown to the Ambassador Theatre and opened there September 27, 1977. Presented by Joseph Papp, this production was directed by Roberto Athayde, setting and costumes were by Santo Loquasto, and lighting was designed by Martin Tudor.

CHARACTERS

Miss Margarida, the lady schoolteacher
One of her students, an actor
The rest of her students, the audience

SET

A teacher's desk
A teacher's chair
And a *green* blackboard

First Class

Good evening to all of you. As you must already know, I am your new teacher. My name is Miss Margarida. I am going to write it on the blackboard so that you can memorize it. [*Writes on board:* Miss Mar-

MISS MARGARIDA

garida.] Now, before we get started I would like to get a little bit acquainted with you. Then I will say a few words about the importance of education. [*Pause.*] Is anyone here named Messiah? And Jesus? No? And Holy Ghost, is there anyone named Holy Ghost in this class? No? Are you sure? [*Pause.*] Good. The Principal had already told me that you were a nice class. There is no good teacher without a good class. Err ... I'm just thinking, this blackboard is a little too far. Can you see it well enough? You in the back? It's very important that everyone sees the greenboard. Miss Margarida is going to write a little word on it to see if you can really see. [*Writes in big letters:*

asshole.] Can you see it? Asshole. The blackboard is actually very important to learn *reading*. And *history*. And *mathe-*

12

matics. And geography. [Goes back to the board and awkwardly sketches a penis.]

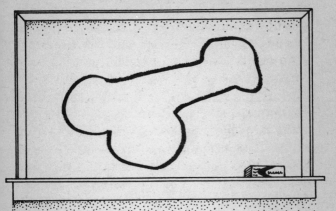

Can you see that? Well, that's a *cape*. Let us say, the Cape of Good Hope. That is *geography*. But, as I was saying, it is necessary to point out and show to you the importance of my function, that is, the importance of *education*. Because, ah ... let's face it, none of you is here of his own accord. You are here because your parents made you. Every one of you with no exception, right? You were all forced to come here willy-nilly. Well, there must be a *good reason* for that. It is a very simple reason. Miss Margarida will explain it to you right away. You have already noticed that that's the way Miss Margarida works: she will explain everything to you right from the beginning. But ... the reason I was saying ... yes, the reason why you are all sitting at your desks without having been able to choose ... the reason is very simple. It's because school is a *second home*. Did any of you choose to be born? Was any of you consulted about the convenience of your being born? No, right? So, that's it, school, being a second home, is the same thing. No one asked your opinion about coming in and now you cannot get out. This is a beautiful truth. You all have to admit that within these walls you have no choice. It is as if you didn't exist. Of course you have to pay, *ça va sans dire....* This is *French*. Miss Margarida is going to write it on the blackboard so that you can learn it. [*Writes:* ÇA VA SANS DIRE.]

That's it. *Ça va sans dire.* That means in French that it is such an obvious truth that you don't even have to mention it. Before today's class is finished I want all of you to say together, "*Ça va sans dire.*" Well ... what was I talking about? What is so obvious that you don't need to say? Oh yes, you all must *pay* for this second home which is school. Every citizen of the country contributes his share for the maintenance of education. In addition to that, in order to be able to get into this class, every one of you was forced to show his ID card to the doorman. Each one of you, just a few minutes ago, had his ID card in hand so that you could prove that you are really allowed to be here. And, as you arrive here, you have to do what was determined by the Principal and what I happen to tell you to do. So, in a way, you were forced in and now you *may not* get out. Unless Miss Margarida tells you to do so. [*Pause.*] I don't want to be *hard* on you. To Miss Margarida, the best class is the class where there is an atmosphere of comprehension, of harmony between the students and the teacher. That same atmosphere of solidarity and tenderness that each one of you finds at home among your dear ones. It is a gift of nature. Everything has its advantages in the world. And to deserve all that, to be grateful for all these things, what should you do? What virtue must you cultivate? *Obedience*. It is the greatest of all qualities. There is a very nice nursery rhyme that goes: "The deserving ones, who are they?/ They are those who obey." I am going to write it on the greenboard so that you memorize it. [*Writes on board:* The de-

serving ones, who are they? They are those who obey.] I want to take advantage of this first class, which is rather an introductory class, to get to know you a little better, for, as you must know, my desire is to know each one of you as if he were my own child. It is to that individual and intensive knowledge of each one of you that Miss Margarida wants to dedicate this first class. I want to take advantage of these verses on the greenboard to tell you something of great importance. Listen carefully: if there is one thing Miss Margarida *does not* tolerate, that is *disobedience*. I don't want to have to interrupt a class because of disciplinary problems. I will not hear of one single case of bad behavior till the end of this term. Without discipline there is no progress, no improvement. At the end of each term there is something called *finals. Exams. Test.* [*Tragic*] I pity he who spends his year bumming around without listening to my advice, without trembling before the responsibility that hangs over his head. You are currently starting your *eighth grade.* Remember this is not anymore fifth grade, nor sixth grade, nor seventh grade. This is *eighth grade.* You must, then, realize that the examinations that await you throughout this period are therefore the most difficult you have ever been confronted with. They will comprise not only the subject matter we will be studying this year, but literally all the information you have been given since you entered school. Failure at any of those exams is a disgrace that can mark your lives forever. So, in this very last year of elementary school, the student who *fails* will see all the doors slammed in his face. It is a whole world of knowledge, it is the bulk of human culture and understanding that becomes suddenly inaccessible to you. And shame, like a black cloak, falls over the name of your family. What can you do in order to spare yourselves such shame? That's what Miss Margarida is here for. You must *obey* Miss Margarida. You must be silent to start with. [*Irritated*] I want to hear a pin drop in this classroom! [*More irritated*] You must be *silent*! [*Getting infuriated, banging ruler on desk*] SILENCE! You must also have a good posture! [*Eyeing severely the public*] Without good posture you can't do anything! You there in the fifteenth row! Where do you think you are? Sit up! What do you take this for? A brothel? [*Pointing at someone*] You are sitting like a prostitute! Did you hear me? [*Pause.*] Is there anybody named Messiah in this classroom? No? What about Jesus? No Jesus either? And Holy Ghost? Any Holy Ghosts in class? None, right? *Fuck you, then!* You can go to hell. Oh yes, the Principal told me what a nice class you are. It is good to teach a *docile* class. I talk, you obey. It's right there on the greenboard: the deserving ones, who are they? They are those who obey. You are all here to *learn*. You are paying to *learn*. That means there are things you don't know. There are *many* things you don't know. In fact, you hardly could say that you know anything at all. That's why you are here. [*Sits at her desk. Gets a fresh start.*] Today's class is *biology*. [*Severe*] Don't you children think it is going to be sex education. Don't you children suppose Miss Margarida is going to teach you the facts of life. [*Evil*] I got news for you. The facts of life are only taught in your senior year of high school. And you are just eighth graders. You better forget about sex education till you are old enough. These things take *maturity*. If you think Miss Margarida is about to teach you how to kiss, how to *fornicate*, you are totally mistaken. Nothing of the sort! I appreciate the fact that you don't know how to do those things. You couldn't possibly. Go learn it in the streets. Don't you kids suppose that Miss Margarida is going to show you her *organs*. The Principal forbade me to take my clothes off in front of you. Not even my tits I can show you. What Miss Margarida is going to teach you is much simpler than that, much more *primary*. The right things for children like you. I'm going to teach you biology with a capital *B*. [*Erases the board.*] There are three great principles in biology. There is one great beginning, a middle that varies in size, and a great end. All of you were *born*. And, which is worse, you were born without choice. You were forced into life. You don't even know *how* you were born. And you know even less *why* you were born. You know nothing at all. [*Irritated*] And still you want to have sex education. You think of nothing but fucking around. [*Cooling*] This is the great beginning principle of biology. The second principle is the middle. That's what you are living right now. It's your teacher, Miss Margarida. It's everything. It's your finals, too. It's high school we all love. It's the diploma you will get if you only do as I tell you. It's everything that is good and beautiful in the world. The third principle is the most important. It is the whole purpose of biology. Miss Margarida must tell you something that you, as children, haven't quite realized yet. But you must know it. It's that each one of you is going to *die*. Every one of you. Miss Margarida is going to write it on the blackboard so that you remember it. [*Writes on board:* ALL OF YOU ARE

ALL OF YOU
ARE GOING TO DIE

GOING TO DIE.] Miss Margarida wants you, for English class, to do a creative paper describing your own funeral in your own words. But remember, it has to be creative. Miss Margarida does not want two single funerals alike in this entire class. Do you understand me? That has a lot to do with *biology*. You don't really know anything about biology. Then how can you pretend to know other things that are still more difficult? You didn't even know you were all going to die! Now you know it. You people really want to know a lot. I know you want to get to the facts of life before the senior year. You wanted Miss Margarida to take off her clothes and be naked in front of you, that's what you really wanted, me, Miss Margarida, stark naked in front of her pupils. What wouldn't the Principal say? There's no way you can hide anything from Miss Margarida. Miss Margarida knows what she is talking about. [*Pause.*] However, Miss Margarida doesn't want to be *hard* on you. Miss Margarida doesn't want you to think that she doesn't love you. All Miss Margarida wants is that each one of you come out of her classes just a little bit *better* than before. Each time you come out of this classroom you will know something that you didn't know before. That's what Miss Margarida really wants. That makes you better prepared to face every obstacle that may be in your way. For there *will* be obstacles in your way, my dear students. Please don't let yourselves be too impressed by the three great principles of biology. There are things much worse than that. History, for example. Do you know what is the great principle of History? Everyone wants to dominate everyone else. Exactly like Miss Margarida dominates you. In this classroom you have no choice: you do what Miss Margarida tells you to do and only when Miss Margarida tells you. And you *pay* for that! In history it's the same thing. Every country wants to have that kind of relationship with all the others. Conclusion: *everyone wants to be Miss Margarida*. I am going to write it on the greenboard so that you can remember it. That's it! I'm your teacher, and you better believe it. And don't you imagine that you can complain to the Principal.... I want every one of you to know that the Principal is on Miss Margarida's side! Miss Margarida here represents the Principal. In a way Miss Margarida *is* the Principal. [*Irritated*] You don't make any decisions in this classroom. Don't you think that just because there is a bell that's going to ring that I have to let you go. You are very much mistaken. I can have the whole class here overtime. The entire class locked up in this classroom copying lines! Five thousand times! That sentence: *Ev-*

eryone wants to be Miss Margarida! You can stay here all night writing! [*Pause.*] Miss Margarida does not want to be hard on you. [*Pause.*] The punishments Miss Margarida sometimes has to give you are really meant as incentive. It's for your own good. You must get acquainted with the hardships of life while you are still young. None of you really knows what hardship is. Sometimes you may think that the worst has passed but you are always mistaken. The worst is always in the future. The worst is always what comes after. That is actually the final principle of biology: all of you will end up buried in the cemetery or else reduced to ashes. This is a very simple truth that Miss Margarida is determined to make you assimilate in this eighth-grade year. You won't be learning that when you are seniors. In the senior year things start changing a little. It's the peak of adolescence! The boys start giving a little more of themselves and the girls start getting wronged. And after that you will never be the same boys and girls that you are here. From then on you'll be only concerned with *fucking and getting fucked* for the rest of your lives. But it's not in *my* classroom that this is going to happen. I want *respect* in this classroom. I want *discipline.* I want *decorum.* You good-for-nothings! Do you know what microbe is? Of course you wouldn't. It's biology, too! They are small animals that kill us and nobody sees them. There are millions of them, they kill thousands of people every day. Everyone knows that but nobody sees anything. Miss Margarida is going to draw a microbe on the blackboard for you. [*Draws a nearly invisible microbe.*] See?

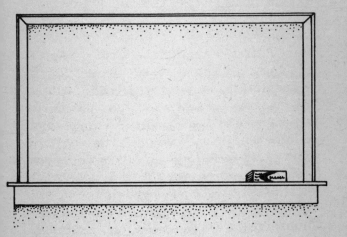

You can't see it. And virus? Do you know what a virus is? It's the same thing as a microbe, only still smaller. Miss Margarida's going to draw you a virus on the blackboard. [*Draws an invisible virus.*]

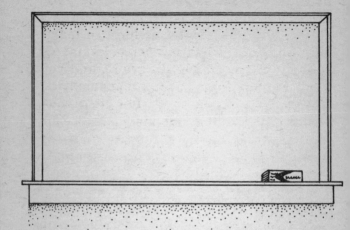

That's what biology is all about. Things just can't be seen that easily. Almost nothing can be seen. Take you people, for example. You can't really see very much. If you could, you wouldn't be paying a fortune to be here in this classroom doing what *I* want. [*Irritated*] Like a bunch of imbeciles. You don't participate in anything in this class. Not one goddamn thing. I talk and you believe whatever I happen to say. I am the fucking teacher here. [*Infuriated*] Silence! SILENCE! *I need silence to work.* I'll ram this greenboard up the ass of the first bastard who opens his mouth! You don't understand anything. Must I repeat everything like a goddamn parrot? If you think I am here at your disposal like a tape recorder, you are very much mistaken. Education is a serious business! You are here to learn. Do you know what *mathematics* is? Of course not! In the eighth grade, and you don't know a thing about mathematics! I'm going to teach you a few instances. *Division*. Now, to divide means that each one of you wants to get more than the others. Do you understand? I am going to teach you on the blackboard to make it perfectly clear. Let us suppose the following problem. In this classroom there are only twelve bananas for thirty-five students. Now, pay attention, please. These thirty-five mouths wanting bananas must therefore *divide* the twelve bananas among themselves. What is going to happen? Well, the strongest student will get eight or nine bananas all for himself. The second strongest will get three or four bananas. And the thirty-three remaining mouths will be left *perfectly without bananas*. That is division. Mathematics is the basis of all the other disciplines. Division is applied in all levels of society. You must learn well your division before you leave elementary school. Now, *equation*. Miss Margarida asks you: what is equation? Obviously you don't know. Miss Margarida realizes that there is not much you do know. In fact, you hardly know anything at all. That's what Miss Margarida is here for. To teach you. Well, equation. Equation is when one thing is *equal* to another. For instance, in our country all men are equal. How can Miss Margarida explain that to you? Well, let's see it on the greenboard. [*Draws a large pot.*] This is our melting pot. That's where

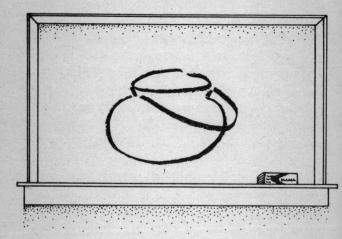

our equation takes place. Suppose there is a red man. Then a white man comes. In this country red and white are equal. As soon as they come together they *melt*. There we have our first equation. Then come the black men and they melt together as soon as they arrive. That is because they are equal and nobody can tell any difference. So, there is red, there is white, and there is black but, as they are equal, nobody can tell the difference. That is so because there is no difference. Miss Margarida cannot see any difference. Is any of you capable of seeing a difference? If any of you notices a difference, please come up to the blackboard. [*An actor who was sitting with the audience now comes onstage. He is extremely awkward. As he approaches he is rudely stopped by Miss Margarida.*] Who told you to come here? What do you think you are doing here? You think you saw any *difference* on the blackboard, right? You want to spoil Miss Margarida's equation, right? [*Furious, loud*] Go immediately back to your desk! Get your ass out of here! [*The student goes back to his seat.*] Arrogant bastard! It's time you people knew your place. How dare you interrupt Miss Margarida when she is teaching equation? You absolutely must learn equation before you are out of grammar school. You are only eighth graders. You better have a good equation background before your freshman year. Adolescence is coming. In a couple of years each one of you will be an *adolescent*. It's the age of doubts. It is the most dangerous age because it's the age when boys and girls run the risk of rebelling against their teachers. They rebel against their second home, which is school. Some go as far as rebelling against their own parents. It's to prevent that that Miss Margarida is here. To *help* you. Miss Margarida wants each one of you to be a happy and well-adjusted human being so that you can make your way on to college. Will you ever understand that? Sometimes you may think that Miss Margarida is against you. You may think that Miss Margarida is out to blow your minds or something. It's not true. Miss Margarida wants each one of you to be a freshman next year. And then a sophomore the following year. That's what Miss Margarida really wants. But for that you must cooperate with Miss Margarida. It's necessary that Miss Margarida feels in you an intense desire to learn. That's all Miss Margarida wants from you. I myself was a student like you are today. Miss Margarida was a model student. Miss Margarida was never punished by her schoolteacher. That is, except once. Miss Margarida will tell you about that so it serves as an example. Miss Margarida was about eight or nine. Miss Margarida was a model student. And guess what Miss Margarida did to be

punished? Nothing! Absolutely nothing!
That was an *injustice*. I'm telling you that
Miss Margarida hadn't done a thing! It
was this bitchy girl friend of Miss Margarida's who did it and Miss Margarida
got the blame in her place. And that little
slut was also named Margarida. [*Hateful,
scornful*] Margarida ... That silly little
bitch did it, and Miss Margarida got
screwed. You hear me? That was an injustice. [*Excited*] It was assembly time.
The entire school was lined up outdoors.
I didn't do a thing! Nothing at all! It was
all her fault, that miserable piece of shit.
You know what she did? She was standing
behind Miss Margarida and she kept rub-
bing herself against Miss Margarida's
back till the teacher saw it and she caught
Miss Margarida instead of that whore
Margarida! She punished Miss Margarida,
who hadn't done a thing. Nothing, do you
hear me? And don't you imagine that
could happen in *my* classroom. Miss Margarida hates injustice. [*Screaming*] Miss
Margarida hates injustice! I'll kill anybody who says I can do injustice. Do you
understand? I'll keep the entire class here
after school just to let you know who you
are dealing with! I'll have you WRITE A
HUNDRED THOUSAND TIMES *"Everyone wants to be Miss Margarida."* You

don't know me! You don't know me at all! You don't know what my habits are! And it's not going to be you who will change my habits! [*Frantic*] I adore my habits! Do you hear me? I adore my habits! You don't mean anything to me. I don't care what you think of me! I don't give a shit! You are a bunch of fairies! This classroom is filled up with queers! Help, queers all over the place! The whole world's full of queers! [*Pause; didactic.*] There are only two kinds of men: *the homosexuals and the faggots*. I'm going to write it on the greenboard so that you memorize it. [*Writes:* There are only two kinds of men:

the homosexuals and the faggots.] But

Miss Margarida doesn't want to be *hard* on you. The same way Miss Margarida teaches you the tough things of life Miss Margarida also teaches you the simple and beautiful things. Miss Margarida teaches you the *poetry* of the world. Things that you also must learn early in life. In spite of everything, my dear students, you *do love Miss Margarida.* You like your teacher. And Miss Margarida also loves you. She *cares* for each one of you. Even though sometimes Miss Margarida has to tell you things that you don't like. This is *poetry.* And this, with everything else, makes up the pleasure of teaching. The satisfaction of having a docile and obedient class like you. I knew the Principal was right when he said you were a nice class. That makes Miss Margarida happy. That makes Miss Margarida tremble with joy. Now you tell Miss Margarida in all sincerity: is there anybody here named *Messiah?* And Jesus? Are you sure? Not one single Jesus? What about Holy Ghosts? No Holy Ghosts either? [*Pause.*] Good. That's the way I like it. An entire school made up of classes all like you would be perfect. That represents *effort* and *work* of your teachers. The least you can do to deserve that is to be grateful. Gratitude is the greatest of all qualities. You also must be grateful to your parents. You wouldn't be here if it wasn't for them. But it is not for gratitude that Miss Margarida is a teacher. Miss Margarida's activities are totally disinterested. This is something I want to make perfectly clear. One day, when you are all adults, you will understand the words of Miss Margarida. Then you will be sorry for all the bad thoughts you had about Miss Margarida. You won't deny that you *do* have bad thoughts about Miss Margarida, will you? WILL YOU? Miss Margarida wants to know *who* of you has the courage to say what he or she thinks about Miss Margarida. [*Irritated*] You are afraid to talk! You won't say a goddamn thing! [*Infuriated*] A bunch of cowards, that's what you are! Go ahead, say it right to my face! You are all full of shit! Who's gonna be first to step forward and say something? You faggots! You morons! I'll kick your stinking balls in! Who's gonna come up here? You're gonna say Miss Margarida is a ballbuster, aren't you? [*Quite beside herself, screaming*] I *am* a fucking ballbuster! And you are all pederasts and bums! You want to say Miss Margarida is a crazy cunt, I know it! Then, fuck you! [*Running hysterically*

34

about the stage] I'm a desperate cunt! I'm gonna castrate all of you. I'll cut off your balls and throw them in the river! What do you take me for? A good-for-nothing? A fucked-up whore? A shithead that everyone pushes around? [*Crying*] You're gonna treat me very well! You're gonna respect me as I respect you! [*Cooling*] You want to make me lose my temper! That's what you are trying to do! You want me to scream! [*Screaming*] I don't need to yell to make myself heard! If you can't hear me, fuck you! You want to make me spend the whole time yelling at you! So that way I teach you less. It won't do any good. I stop this class when *I* want. Don't you imagine that just because there is a bell that's gonna ring that I have to let you go. I'm gonna teach you *all of it* even if I have to keep you here all night! You must come out of here knowing something about biology. Do you know what *evolution* is? Of course you don't. You don't know anything! So, evolution is *nothing*. It does not exist. *It's always the same thing*. Nothing changes! That's what evolution is: NOTHING! Everything is always the same crap. I'm going to write it on the greenboard so that you remember it. [*Writes:* Evolution is nothing.] And *revolution*, do you know what it is? Of course not. It's two times evolution. Two times nothing, *nothing*! It's nothing at all! [*Writes on board:* Revolution is nothing.] See? All that is nothing. There is just nothing to it! Nothing at all! [*Obsessed by negatives*] Not this, not that, not anything! There's nothing to anything. You people can't do anything in this classroom. All I'll let you do is *nothing*. You are nothing but children. A bunch of morons! You do what Miss Margarida tells you to do. A bunch of silly little fairies, that's what you are! [*Grimaces and apes the audience like a mentally retarded child.*] Morons! In eighth grade and you think you are already seniors! Ha! I could beat the shit out of any of you. [*Pause.*] Miss Margarida doesn't like fooling around. Getting an education is the most serious responsibility you have at your age. It is not only for your own future but for the future of your country. You people are very lucky; in this classroom every one of you is at least semiliterate. With just a little more effort any of you can reach full literacy level. Why not make that effort? Everything is in your hands! He who can read is much better off in life than he who cannot read. You must take your education seriously. That's what you are going to live on. That's what your children one day are going to feed on. Just think for one minute, my dear students, the progress that we could make in this classroom if only all of you could read fluently? Miss Margarida doesn't mean to say that you cannot read. Miss Margarida knows that you can read. [*Stimulating*] But why not read *even better*? Fluently! Isn't that a good reason for us to make an effort? [*Coy*] All of us! Together! Cooperation is the secret! [*Pause.*] Well, I think we have already talked enough. We have lots of things to learn. This dialogue between pupils and the teacher is necessary, no doubt about that, but some *theory* is also needed. Practice alone is useless. What really puts things together is theory. Now that we are a little better acquainted, in spite of some disciplinary problems, since I've succeeded in imparting some basic notions of biology to you, let's go into biology itself. Anyway, what is biology? Biology is the science of life. Of other people's lives. The science of our own life is called *medicine*. I've already taught you the three great principles of biology. You've already forgotten all of it. They are the beginning, the middle, and the end. We cannot go any further into the beginning because it involves the facts of life. You will only learn the facts of life when you are *seniors*. Now, the *middle*. The middle of biology is life itself. Which of you never indulged in *masturbation*? The ones who never masturbated come up to the greenboard, immediately. The others, the masturbators, remain seated at your desks. Don't be ashamed. Don't be bashful. Don't blush. [*Once more the awkward student comes onstage.*] Hey you. What do you think you are doing there? Nobody was supposed to come up here now. You look like an idiot. You mean you never played with your thing? And *why* didn't you? You can tell Miss Margarida. Miss Margarida thinks you haven't got a thing. You can go right back to your desk. It was all a mistake; you weren't supposed to come up here to begin with. [*The student moves back to his desk.*] Cute, isn't he? [*Pause.*] Well, well, well, what was I lecturing you about? You can bet your ass it wasn't the facts of life. You might as well forget about that. Miss Margarida has a responsibility toward our program. Miss Margarida is not like some teachers who wander off the subject, tell stories, reminiscences, things that have nothing to do with the subject matter. I myself had a teacher like that. She couldn't get through a class without telling some sort of romantic story. She knew everything about everyone's life. She was a good teacher, though, in spite of being so dispersive. She was an intelligent woman, that Miss Margarida. Yes, she was also named Margarida. She had a clear preference for Miss Margarida. You know, some teachers always have a pet student. She used to call Miss Margarida "alter ego." She had a very strong temper, that Miss Margarida. Once, in phys. ed. class, she hit a kid in the wrong place and he got crippled for life. He became sterile. And what a sense of humor that Miss Margarida had! She had this amazing joke she used to tell us at religious class. It was something about a bull in a corral that got visited by a sparrow. It had some zoomorphic subtlety to it.... You don't know what zoomorphic means, of course. ... Well, forget it, it's Latin. But what was the joke? Oh yes, the bull ... the sparrow ... I can't remember it. ... All I can remember is the punch line: the sparrow sucks the bull ... and the bull sucks the sparrow.... Oh, what an extraordinary woman was that Miss Margarida. She only had that one shortcoming, which was really quite unforgivable. She couldn't give a lecture without interrupting with hearsay, blablabla and what not. She would say that in her own time children had more respect for their teachers. There was more sense of obedience. Actually, Miss Margarida had a perfect class. Miss Margarida is not saying this just because she belonged to the class of Miss Margarida but, let's face it, Miss Margarida was among the best students of Miss Margarida's. Miss Margarida always made very complimentary comments about Miss Margarida and Miss Margarida always lived up to Miss Margarida's expectations. Miss Margarida only wishes that Miss Margarida could have a class like that of Miss Margarida's with all students like Miss Margarida! [*Pause.*] Everything changed from Miss Margarida's time to now. There is no respect for teachers now. Well, at least the teaching methods seem to have improved a little bit. Things are more direct. What teacher nowadays could indulge in digression? Or even a slight change in the sequence of events? Everything has to be taught straight from the textbook. But don't imagine that just because of that I'm forced to stop the class when the bell rings. I'm the boss in this classroom. [*Pause.*] Well. [*Pause.*] Miss Margarida is actually responsible for most of the progress in teaching methods over the past decades. Miss Margarida created her own original teaching method. It's called "Hamburger-Sudamerikanische Dampfschiffahrtsgesellschaft." This is German. That means, in English, Margaridian Method for Instant Erudition. Miss Margarida's method is based on the idea that one should learn for the sake of teaching and teach for the sake of learning. Miss Margarida's method is especially meant for mass education. Miss Margarida gives private tutoring in this method for only twenty bucks an hour. It's the ideal thing for the postindustrial society. Miss Margarida has herself composed a little anthem that stands for the ideals of Miss Margarida's method. Let's hear Miss Margarida's composition. [*Sings the following words with a simple and ridiculous melody.*] "Let us sing, let us pray/Miss Margarida's way!" What's the matter? It looks like you didn't appreciate Miss Margarida's work. You didn't like Miss Margarida's anthem, isn't that so? You are not very sensitive to music, are you? Do you realize what you just heard? That was a masterpiece of our hymnary. It can stand side by side with the very best pages in its genre. You don't know what *genre* means, of course not! I got news for you. No one will leave this room without knowing Miss Margarida's song *by heart*. Now, *sing it all together.* [*Trying to conduct the audience*]

Sing it: one, two three. [*Singing*] Let us sing, let us pray ... [*Furious*] Nobody is singing. A bunch of morons, that's what you are! Start singing immediately! One, two, three! [*Singing*] Let us sing, let us pray ... Sing, you bastards! I want everybody singing in the fucking classroom! A bunch of irresponsible *slobs*, that's what you are! I'm wasting my time with you! I know you want me to teach the facts of life. I shall *never* teach you the facts of life! Never never never never never! Don't you motherfuckers suppose I'm going to undress in front of you. You are here to learn, not to have fun. There is nothing funny in what I am saying. [*Long pause.*] I've already said I don't want to be hard on you. Miss Margarida doesn't like to be tough. Miss Margarida has always said there is only one way to intellectual betterment: that is an atmosphere of comprehension, cooperation, and understanding. And that is also the only way you can get into high school. There has to be understanding in this classroom. [*Stops and sniffs something in the air.*] Anyway, what is understanding? It is the essential element of progress. Without understanding there can be no progress. This is something Miss Margarida wants to make

43

perfectly clear. [*Stops again and sniffs more. A stink bomb has been set by a rebellious pupil and its terrible smell pervades the entire classroom.*] No! It is not possible. Someone has blown a stink bomb in this classroom! Who did it? I'll kill, I'll strangle whoever did that! I swear. I'll murder the son of a bitch! You can't beat Miss Margarida! Don't imagine you can beat Miss Margarida! [*Choking*] You bastards! You're evil! You are no good. You'll be damned to the last bastard! [*The bell rings loudly for recess.*] RECESS, YOU MOTHERFUCKERS! Everyone out of the fucking classroom! [*Lights on for intermission.*] Everyone out of here! You have twenty minutes to examine your conscience. I want the guilty one at the greenboard after recess. He will never forget the way he will be punished. Out, every stinking brat! [*Exit Miss Margarida always yelling and mumbling.*] Bums! That's all I needed! A stink bomb right in the middle of biology! Things are not gonna stay like this! I swear to God I'll get you back for that.

RECESS

Second Class

[*Miss Margarida enters and goes toward her desk. Looks back dramatically to the greenboard to see if there are any confessors to the stink bomb. Sees nobody and visibly forgets all about it and addresses the classroom in a very serious manner, almost contrite.*] Miss Margarida had prepared *catechism* for this second class. Such a class would approach a theme of general interest which is, so to speak, the backbone of our religious faith. As you must already know, there was a great *passion* in the life of our Lord Jesus Christ. Well, it's no use going into it since we can't go very far.... The sad truth is that because of your insubordination you learned absolutely nothing in the last class. This class therefore will be once more a *biology class*. [*Threatening*] And you better like it. You are going to have as much biology as it takes to make you learn. If necessary, all classes will be biology classes till the end of the year! Miss Margarida won't have her subject interrupted. What is started must be taken to the bitter end. I bet you thought you were gonna have sex education for catechism. You were hoping there would be the *facts of life* in Jesus Christ's passion. You are very much mistaken. In Jesus' time there was no pornography. Things happened by miracle. It wasn't this mess you see nowadays. And as for the facts of life, it's no use insisting on it. You'll get that only in the senior year. And by the way, I want to tell you something very serious. Very, very serious. I've noticed that nobody has confessed his guilt about the stink bomb affair. Don't imagine I have forgotten that. While you were eating your lunch Miss Margarida got sick in the Principal's office. Miss Margarida coughed and choked and vomited right in front of the Principal. Miss Margarida almost died because of the misbehavior of one single student. You must all examine your conscience. I want the guilty one to come spontaneously over to the greenboard and confess. You have to learn how to *confess* when you do something as serious as this. You must all examine your conscience. [*Pause.*] Well, Miss Margarida doesn't want to insist. Miss Margarida will leave that to your own discretion. Let's go back to our subject matter. [*Opens a shutter that hides a human skeleton natural size.*] Here is our skeleton! One day in the future each one of you will look exactly like this. But nobody will be able to see you because you will be buried. It is because of this impossibility of seeing our friends as skeletons that the *bony science* was created. To begin with, what is a bone? Bones are the *hard* parts of the human body. Which does not mean that anything hard or likely to become so is a bone. One must always bear in mind that in medicine all rules are confirmed by countless exceptions. For instance: in the beginning all bones were soft. The fetus is basically a soft thing. [*Makes a repulsed face.*] As it gets a little bigger it starts getting a little harder. It gets harder and harder as time passes. This notion of hardness is one of the most important things in biology. Now, pay attention to Miss Margarida's words. Now Miss Margarida asks you: Which

one would be the most important part?
The head? But just think that a head
could never live on its own. Would it be
the trunk? Or the limbs? You are a bunch
of dummies, aren't you? Considering the
whole of the human creature, neither
the head nor the trunk nor the limbs
have the slightest importance. [*Suddenly
mad*] All three are totally useless! Totally worthless! Do you think Miss Margarida is here to exalt the human body?
You're very much mistaken. You probably
think Miss Margarida is one of those *he-
donists*. Do you know what a hedonist is?
Of course not! You don't know anything
whatsoever! Hedonist is *Greek*. It means
"the sensual woman"! [*Infuriated*] Miss
Margarida doesn't give a damn, do you
understand? Miss Margarida *does not give
a shit*. That skeleton is *your* skeleton:
Miss Margarida hasn't got a skeleton!
Miss Margarida *has never been hard.*
[*Pointing to the skeleton*] Don't imagine
that Miss Margarida mingles with that
kind of people. [*Feeling her own arms*]
You see? Miss Margarida has no skeleton!
Miss Margarida's arms are absolutely
flexible! [*Doing a weird belly dance to
demonstrate her flexibility*] Flexible! Miss
Margarida hasn't a single bone. And before I forget: Miss Margarida does yoga.

Miss Margarida knows yoga. And Miss Margarida *levitates*, too. One of these days Miss Margarida will lecture you on levitation. Miss Margarida *rises*. Miss Margarida can rise any moment she wants to. You folks think Miss Margarida is just theory. You are badly mistaken. Miss Margarida practices. Miss Margarida understands the vibrations of the body just as well as the vibrations of the mind. Miss Margarida always did sensitivity training on her students long before anybody thought of that. Miss Margarida doesn't need to think: Miss Margarida *feels*. Miss Margarida participates. Miss Margarida is constantly *reaching out* to the world. One must *reach out* to the world around oneself in order to have a sound mind. Miss Margarida also reaches out to the world of trees and plants. They also have a language of their own. And Miss Margarida understands that language. And the same thing happens with the mineral world. Rocks also have a language of their own. And Miss Margarida understands that language. Miss Margarida can feel the *rocks* breathing in nature. This is *ecology*. Miss Margarida won't lecture you on ecology: Miss Margarida *is* ecology. Miss Margarida also understands the animal world. Miss

Margarida understands the language animals talk. Each species has a particular way of life that must be respected and understood. Miss Margarida is the pioneer of a new movement that will change the destiny of mankind. Miss Margarida is going to expose a new kind of social injustice that has existed unsuspected to this very day. It is the most shameful of all social injustices: it is the nefarious injustice that is carried out against our brother *animals*. With what right do we women consider ourselves superior to the other species? There is no scientific proof that a woman is basically superior to a bull. With what right therefore do we ill-treat and devour the bull? *Miss Margarida is with the bull!* Each one of you must consider this problem. There can be no justice in the world as long as there is no equality among the species. A pig has the same right to life as each one of you! Taking the freedom of pigs and confining them in pigsties is a *crime* of which you must be ashamed. Miss Margarida is a vegetarian. Miss Margarida wants each one of you to become a vegetarian from now on. That will be our effort to do justice. The animals want no charity, they want *justice*. And justice is equality in power and in pride. Miss Margarida rejects the theory that some animals are more equal than others. A cheese worm that feeds exclusively on cheese and actually lives inside the cheese has obviously much more right to that cheese than a housewife. Miss Margarida wants you to think about that. Whenever you find a cockroach or any bugs floating in your soup do not feel uneasy about your roach or your bugs: *share* your soup with those animals. Miss Margarida has fought all her life for these ideals. Difficulties are great and many. There is a great deal of incomprehension. There are those who claim that animals are inferior by nature and are incapable of following our civilization. It is not true. Science proves that all species are essentially equal. And that is the basis of Miss Margarida's animal liberation. The differences are due to external circumstances. They are due to the *climate*. They are due to the centuries of oppression and exploitation that animals have suffered from mankind. The difference is always due to something that can be changed. And that is the great ambition of Miss Margarida's: to change. To change everything! Change the mind of each one of you. What would be the good of Miss Margarida's authority over you if she couldn't modify your minds? Miss

Margarida molds you. When Miss Margarida says you must do something it means that you just *have* to do it. You must obey willy-nilly. Whether you like it or not. [*Irritated*] In this classroom you do exactly as *I* say. No more, no less. Miss Margarida can send any of you to the Principal's office. There are very few students Miss Margarida has already sent to the Principal's office: *none of them has ever come back*. Miss Margarida does not know what happened to them, but Miss Margarida can guarantee you that nothing good happened to them. You are here to obey. You are here to learn. That means you don't know anything. Nothing at all! [*Getting progressively infuriated*] I won't tolerate any disciplinary problems in this classroom. What kind of an education you think you've got? You are incapable of comprehending the effort and the dedication of a teacher. You are a bunch of street urchins! Ignoramuses! Bums! In eighth grade you know *nothing at all*! You don't know the first thing about biology. You don't recognize your own skeleton. [*Starts dismantling the skeleton, revealing some violence. Rips an arm off. Hesitates. Shows an almost erotic interest for the arm. Gives the impression she is going to start lecturing furiously but says nothing.*

Places the arm on the floor and goes back to the skeleton. Handles the skeleton absent-mindedly and ad lib and eventually attacks the skeleton, reducing it to a heap of bones on the floor. Goes back to her desk. Restarts calm but severe.] Now, since we were talking about classroom behavior, is there anybody named Messiah in this classroom? No? And Jesus? No Jesus either? Are you sure? And Holy Ghosts? Is there anyone named Holy Ghost? No? [*Sadistic*] *Fuck you, then.* [*Pause.*] Miss Margarida is fed up with you. I know, you are gonna say that you, too, are fed up with Miss Margarida. That's it. It's because biology is a pain in the ass, this goddamn school is a pain in the ass, LIFE IS A PAIN IN THE ASS! I'm going to write it down so that you won't forget it. [*Writes on board:* Life is a pain in the ass!] All

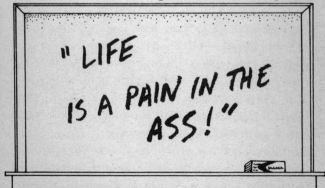

Miss Margarida wants is to make these classes as painless as possible. But you must cooperate for that. That cooperation consists mainly in two things. The first one is that you do not react in any manner to what Miss Margarida says. This condition you boys and girls have fulfilled perfectly well. So far you have been perfectly passive, nothing pointing to the idea that you might be able to produce one single thought. The Principal had told Miss Margarida you were a pretty good class. This makes Miss Margarida happy. It really satisfies Miss Margarida. The second necessary thing in this cooperation program is something Miss Margarida has already told you but which is always convenient to point out again: that is a blind obedience to Miss Margarida. You children here within these walls have no right to anything. You are actually entitled to nothing at all. You are just students of Miss Margarida's. You must understand what you are so that you can behave accordingly. Good behavior is essential to a growing boy or girl. Just think all you could get from your parents if you just behaved well. And even from Miss Margarida. Who knows if Miss Margarida wouldn't give you a little sex education class if just you improved your manners? Think about that! Miss Margarida could perhaps open up her blouse just a little bit and show her tits to you. Just think about that! Miss Margarida could pull her skirt up just a tiny bit for you. [*Giggles with pathos.*] But all that is only if you *work* hard. There is no prize without dedication and sacrifice. Miss Margarida would like to reward you. It all depends on you. Who knows if one day Miss Margarida wouldn't strip and be in the nude in front of you? But for that you must study. You must work hard. There is much to learn and very little time. You are many, Miss Margarida is one. Miss Margarida is unique. There is no way Miss Margarida can pass on to you everything she knows. Biology is the science of life. It comprehends everything that exists. Miss Margarida believes everything is alive. That is the real gist of Miss Margarida's biology. To prepare you for life. Miss Margarida will now enter a subject the importance of which cannot be exaggerated. You all talk a lot about it but there is very little that you actually know about it. Miss Margarida is talking about *narcotics. Drugs.* They are the greatest threat that hangs over the head of each one of you. It's the greatest threat that hangs over the heads of all young people all over the world. [*Pause.*] What is a drug? A drug, my dear students, is something that kills. Something that destroys. It is the tragedy of being destroyed by one's own actions, slowly but steadily. It is suicide. In today's world, drugs are the utmost preoccupation of all parents. And also of all teachers and educators. Miss Margarida wants to lecture you about that. To illuminate you. To guide you toward knowledge and courage to face the danger. The danger, my dear students, is literally everywhere. Just about on every street corner. Among all deadly drugs the deadliest is the *Cannabis sativa.* It is vulgarly known as marijuana. Therefore, if ever one of you sees a *Cannabis sativa,* do turn away from that *Cannabis sativa.* It is the most dangerous of all drugs because it leads directly to the use of other drugs and throws its victims in the bottomless abyss of promiscuity and crime. To let the *Cannabis sativa* into the respiratory channels is the greatest disgrace that can happen to a person. And when Miss Margarida says drugs, it's not only the *Cannabis sativa.* There are countless of these evil substances that will seduce the adolescent and throw him down the pit of vice. They are the awful cortege of drugs that follow the *Cannabis sativa*. There's *heroin*. There's *morphine*. All those poisons that God created in order to test our obedience. And you children are even more exposed than adults to the dangers of vice. Miss Margarida brought you today a slide documentary that shows the effects of addiction in the life of a student. There will be no doubts left after seeing the slides Miss Margarida brought for you. You'll have a clear picture of the tragedy right on the screen. Miss Margarida wants to make a point of answering every question that you can possibly conceive relating to the problem of narcotics. Do not hesitate to interrupt Miss Margarida. Miss Margarida will answer *all the questions* regardless of how stupid they are. [*She prepares the machine, the screen, and gets ready to start.*] Here we are. This series of slides aims at showing the progression of *Cannabis sativa* addiction in the life of an adolescent student. [*Turns the first slide on. It shows an all-American boy, blond and incredibly healthy.*] Here you see a healthy young man in the prime of his adolescence. This young man, up to the day this photo was taken, had lived a wholesome and happy life full of joy, studying and playing among his companions. A virtuous life, sober, with moderate masturbation. Till one day, out of curiosity, just not to be different from the others, our young man smoked a cigarette of *Cannabis sativa*. [*Changes slides; the same young man appears well dressed, at a party, holding a glass of scotch with some sophistication.*] That was the beginning of the end. At first the cannabis had no effect. A few days later, still at the insistence of his friends, our unexperienced hero smoked a second cigarette of *Cannabis sativa*. [*Changes slides, and there appears the same young man holding a bottle of scotch at a bar's counter in a scene of mild drunkenness.*] This time he got his effect all right. The harm was done. Next time it wasn't at a party or even in the street that he smoked the *Cannabis sativa*. [*Changes slides to scenes of severe alcoholic intoxication and many bottles of whiskey.*] It was in the solitude of his own room that he now smoked the *Cannabis sativa!* Alone with the drug that caused his damnation. That, my dear students, is the awful fate of those who will let themselves be dragged down the road of drug addiction. It's an unfathomable abyss that leads rapidly to weakness and death. [*Changes slides to same character lying on the floor surrounded by countless empty bottles of scotch.*] Miss Margarida wants each one of you to promise her you won't be chained down to any such vice. You must be forever warned: the illness of the *Cannabis sativa* starts from within. It starts in the lungs. Miss Margarida is going to show you what a healthy lung should look like. [*Changes slides to a close-up of a normal lung.*] Look at the beauty of that lung! Clear! Translucent! Who wouldn't want to have such a nice lung? Now Miss Margarida is going to show you what the *Cannabis sativa* can do to an adolescent lung. Look at this other lung totally affected by the drug. [*Changes slides to the very same normal lung.*] Look at the terrible condition of this lung! See the difference? Look at the holes! Just look at those holes! [*Laughing with gusto*] Look at the poisoned spots, the parts already degenerated! Did you see the difference? Let's take another look at the healthy lung ... [*Changes to same lung.*] ... and now again the lung rotting with *Cannabis sativa.* [*Changes to same lung.*] Miss Margarida wants all of you to be aware of the risks you take. That's what school is made for. That's what Miss Margarida is made for. To alert you. To show you the reality of things and force you to act in the right manner. But this commitment of teachers to organize their students' private lives is a pretty recent thing. Don't imagine it was like this in the old times. How things really have changed! This fabulous progress! In Miss Margarida's time, teachers were purely theoretical. They thought they could transmit knowledge and experience by words. Thank God all that has changed. At those times teachers didn't even know how to give their students psychological assistance when they needed it most. Miss Margarida herself was to an extent a victim of this lack of orientation. Miss Margarida is also human. Miss Margarida can make mistakes too. Miss Margarida was also an eighth grader like each of you. Miss Margarida had all the problems you have today. Miss Margarida will never forget a great problem in Miss Margarida's life. A great phase. Miss Margarida had a little girl friend in elementary school. She was a dyke. One fine day she started eyeing Miss Margarida. Miss Margarida got very worried. Miss Margarida was very, very perturbed. This Margarida girl stood right behind Miss Margarida when the whole school used to sing the national anthem out in the patio. She kept touching Miss Margarida. She actually liked Miss Margarida. Do you understand? She would start feeling up Miss Margarida. Miss Margarida got very, very worried. Very, very perturbed. Nowadays nothing of the sort could possibly happen. Nowadays it is part of a teacher's job to provide for the morality of his students just as well as for their intellects. That's what Miss Margarida is for. To illuminate. To prepare. To provide for. To mold each one of you. Your personality is like a shapeless piece of soft clay. It can take any form in the hands of Miss Margarida. You still have no definite personality. You are going to improve little by little. It goes slowly. Little by little. If you make a strong effort, everyone will pass the examinations. Next year you will be all in junior high! Your horizons will get larger and larger. But for that you must follow the instructions of Miss Margarida. You must follow them blindly. That's what you are here for. You pay for that. You don't want to waste your time. What would your dad and mom think if Miss Margarida didn't make you obey? Always remember the stanza: "The deserving ones, who are they?/They are those who obey." You must understand that here you have no active voice. You are in the hands of Miss Margarida. You will not be heard about anything at all. It is as if you didn't exist. But of course you have to pay for it. You have no choice. All of you must present your ID cards to the doorman. [*Getting irritated*] You don't make any decisions here. Miss Margarida gives no permission that anything is done without special permission. Miss Margarida won't let you do anything. Not this, not that, nothing at all! Miss Margarida will not feel sorry for you. Miss Margarida has no pity for rebels. Miss Margarida knows when she must be ruthless with you. [*Getting infuriated*] Where do you think you are? In a fucking whorehouse? You are very mistaken. I want a lot of *respect* in this classroom! You are a bunch of parasites. Don't imagine you can push me around. I am the boss in the goddamn classroom! You're gonna learn biology even if I have to beat the shit out of you. You think you're gonna get sex education, right? You wanna see Miss Margarida's *cunt*, that's what you really want! Fuck you, licentious bastards! I'll shove that skeleton up your ass! Silence! I WANT SILENCE! Fuck the biology class! To hell with the goddamn school! Fuck you! [*Great pause;*

after pause, quite unexpectedly] In California it's the same shit. [*Pause.*] Miss Margarida doesn't want to be hard on you. Miss Margarida doesn't want to humiliate you. Miss Margarida is here to help you. All Miss Margarida wants is your happiness. Miss Margarida likes you. [*Coy*] And you do like Miss Margarida. Miss Margarida knows there are many things you would like to say but that you don't because you are just too passive. [*With coy tenderness*] You are perhaps a little impotent, too. Miss Margarida knows that. Miss Margarida understands that. [*Motherly*] Miss Margarida wants to help you not to say anything. Miss Margarida wants to adjust you so that you don't even have anything you'd like to say. That's the way Miss Margarida prepares you for life. Because in life nobody really has anything to say. You must not be discouraged when Miss Margarida scolds you. That's the only way you can absorb the true essence of Miss Margarida's teachings. Miss Margarida's harshness hurts Miss Margarida herself more than it hurts you. Miss Margarida is like a second mother to you. [*Candor*] Miss Margarida wants to help you to be impotent. You know, like, Miss Margarida is your second mama. But you must cooperate with Miss Margarida. That's the only way we can keep up with our school's standards. Miss Margarida helps you. And you help Miss Margarida. You must give a little more thought to the importance of your exams. It's your admission to ninth grade that is at stake. And remember: if you don't make it to ninth grade you may as well forget about tenth grade. And if you don't enter tenth grade there's no way you could aspire to entering eleventh grade. And if you don't reach your junior year you *do not* reach your senior year. And if you don't finish your senior year that means you didn't even go through high school. And if you couldn't go through high school you may as well forget about college. And if you forget about college you couldn't possibly dream of a master's degree. And you'll never be graduate students and you'll never get a Ph.D. And without your Ph.D., my dear students ... that means you'll never be doctors. [*Sad to have come to the progression's end*] This is the sad reality. And you children must learn that reality. Many are called but few are chosen. Miss Margarida wants to see you all on the right path. It is a tough path. It is a path full of hardships and traps. It is a path full of pitfalls. It is, however, a path that leads to a doctor's degree. [*Sadistic*] Miss Margarida longs to see you as doctors and lawyers and business people. And you will also get married one day. Miss Margarida rejoices when she thinks about that. It makes Miss Margarida tremble with joy. [*There comes onstage the same awkward student of the previous times.*] Who do you think you are? Nobody told you to come here. You can go right back to your desk, you hear me? It was all a mistake: go right back to your desk. [*The student numbly starts back to his desk.*] Just a minute, son. Come back here. Miss Margarida has got something to show you. [*As he gets near, Miss Margarida suddenly grabs him and delivers a fantastic ju-jitsu coup that ends with Miss Margarida triumphantly on top of the prostrate victim. He finally manages to escape the teacher and scurries back to his desk.*] You better learn your lesson now, you shithead! Don't you get your ass near me! Idiotic bastard! Moron! [*Pause. Restarts with a cold, professional air.*] Nowadays nothing can be done without technique. Each one of our acts requires a fair amount of knowledge so that they can be carried out. We Americans call that "know-how." Miss Margarida will write this on the blackboard so that you won't forget it.

[*Writes on board:* know-how.] Nothing

can be done without a certain amount
of know-how. The reason is very simple.
Without it, people wouldn't quite know
just *how* to do what they want to do.
There is only one way to face that problem. That is to have a complete knowledge of all the possibilities of action and
of all the possibilities that each one of
those possibilities has to offer. Miss Margarida, for instance, would never start
any action without pondering on every
possibility and sub-possibility. Suppose,
for example, that Miss Margarida wants
to take a walk, starting from Miss Margarida's apartment. Miss Margarida

takes her elevator and rides down to the
entrance hall. Once in the street Miss
Margarida has to make her first decision:
Miss Margarida must choose between
turning left or turning right. Suppose Miss
Margarida made a right turn. Soon
Miss Margarida will find the intersection
of Miss Margarida's street and the next
street to the right, offering therefore
three new directions for Miss Margarida's
walk. Among many others, Miss Margarida has thus gotten the following possibilities: [*The whole of the walk demonstra-
tion should be done on the greenboard.*] 1)

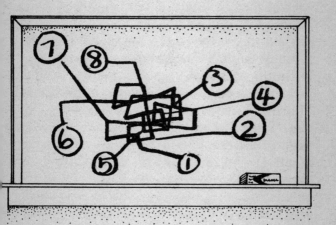

Cross the street and continue in the same
direction on the same sidewalk. 2) Make

a sharp left. 3) Cross the street to the left and then continue in the same direction perpendicularly to the original direction. 4) Cross the street to the left and then continue in the opposite direction perpendicularly to the original direction. 5) Cross the street to the left and then cross it again to the right and proceed in the original direction on the opposite sidewalk. 6) Cross the street to the left and then make another left and follow the direction opposite to the original direction on the opposite sidewalk. 7) Cross the street straight ahead and then make a left and then another left, finally making a right turn and following to the right perpendicularly to the original direction. 8) The eighth possibility is going right back home and calling it a day. . . . As you see, we found eight equally valid possibilities for our stroll. No matter which of these possibilities Miss Margarida chooses, it will lead Miss Margarida to another intersection. Possibility number one would take Miss Margarida to the northeastern corner of Miss Margarida's block, where Miss Margarida would find eight more possibilities. Possibility number two, which consists in making a sharp left, would invariably lead to the northeastern corner of the block following Miss

Margarida's block to the south. This second possibility alone offers Miss Margarida eight more possibilities for her walk. If Miss Margarida followed that making all left turns, Miss Margarida would end up standing on the corner four blocks away from Miss Margarida's facing toward the left. And if Miss Margarida follows that second possibility making all *right* turns, Miss Margarida would end up standing on a corner four blocks away from Miss Margarida's facing toward the right. In either case that means 128 new possibilities to be considered. Each one of those leading Miss Margarida to eight new possibilities to be considered. So, 128 times 8. Let's multiply it quickly. [*Calculates on greenboard.*] There! We've got

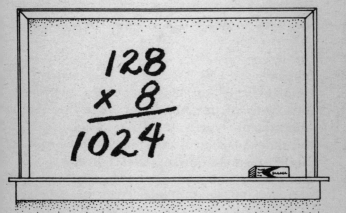

1,024 street corners where Miss Margarida would arrive and which would offer Miss Margarida 8,192 possibilities to be considered. Summing up: Miss Margarida found twenty-four billion, seven hundred thirteen million, four hundred thirty-three thousand, five hundred eleven possibilities for her stroll! [*Writes on board:*

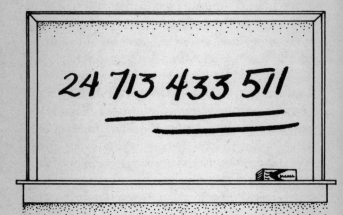

24713433511.] Miss Margarida, before going out of her apartment, studies and learns and weighs each one of those possibilities! Miss Margarida knows precisely the mechanism, the structure, the scheme, the content, the gist, the kernel, the core of that stroll. Otherwise Miss

Margarida would never venture out her door. Method, my dear students, is the only thing that leads to efficiency. Miss Margarida is perfectly aware of the fact that other people have taken and do take walks without any of those precautions. That's their problem. I hope they get lost wandering all over the goddamn city. They will pass each street corner *without knowing* what they are going to do at the next corner or what they could have done at the corner before. To hell with them! Miss Margarida won't set foot outside her apartment without being absolutely sure of each one of her movements! Miss Margarida *chooses*! Miss Margarida *decides*! Miss Margarida *determines*! Miss Margarida can have no surprises, Miss Margarida *foresees*. That is the path, my dear students! One must *know*. Know everything. You understand that? It isn't going to be now in the middle of the twentieth century that man will give up knowledge. Thousands of years of experience! Thousands of years of sacrifice! Thousands of years of culture! Thousands of years of civilization! What for? Many have put this question. The greatest minds in history have asked this question. And Miss Margarida found the answer. The answer is: *just to know*. Just to know what it is all about. All the sacrifices and efforts during thousands of years are just to know what it is all about! And that's what Miss Margarida wants to teach you. What things really are. You want to know what things really are? Things are *adjectives*! Things are big and small, tiny and huge, horrendous, ridiculous, gorgeous, fake and true, new and tough, old and evil and beautiful, red like blood! That's what things really are: *adjectives*. No problem at all! You hear me? Everything is an adjective! And if you want to know just *how* things are what they are there is no problem either! Miss Margarida found the answer! The *way* things are, the manner, the form, all that is *adverb*. You hear me? Adverb! Things are calmly, firstly, obviously, specially, increasingly, terribly, brotherly, tastefully, wonderfully, desperately, inevitably, tragically, eternally! Did you hear me? That's the way things really are! Everything has the same way of being: ADVERB. Everything is an adverb! No problem at all! [*Miss Margarida is more and more excited and talks faster and faster.*] And you wanna know what things do to one another? No problem here either. What things and people do is always verb. Nobody ever did anything that wasn't a verb! *There* is the explanation. You hear me? Everything that is done is bound to be verb! It is the verb to make, the verb to take, the verb to fake, the verb to like, the verb to strike, the verb to laugh, and the verb to cough, the verb to eat and sleep and eat and sleep, the verb to doubt, the verb to play, the verb to stay and obey, the verb to want and the verb to plant and to shit and to bullshit, the verb to love, to lose, to forget, the verb to live! [*Pause. Miss Margarida is nearly hysterical. Restarts slower for crescendo.*] The verb to pass, the verb to last, the verb to cost, the verb to come, the verb to hurt, the verb to heal, the verb to kill, the verb to fill, to dwindle and worsen and prove and improve and postpone, the verb to fear, the verb to die, the verb to dream! [*Miss Margarida is frantic.*] It's all verb! You hear me? It's all verb! That's what things do. Things *verb* one another! And you know what gets all this verb? You know what gets the adverbs and the adjectives? The *nouns.* The substances! The things! Business! Transactions! Classrooms! Schoolteachers! It's Miss Margarida herself! Everything! Miss Margarida is a noun! Everything has a name, there is no problem at all! There is nothing without a name, that's the explanation! Now anybody can see it! The explanation of everything! Nouns, verbs, adverbs, adjectives! Miss Margarida found the answer! Everything is in Miss Margarida's hands! Miss Margarida is the teacher. Miss Margarida is the boss! Miss Margarida bosses the verbs! Miss Margarida tells the adjectives what to do! Miss Margarida can put them all together and make an entire sentence! A PARAGRAPH! Miss Margarida makes a whole paragraph! It's my paragraph, you hear me? *My* sentences! All sentences in this classroom are Miss Margarida's! About any subjects! About *every* subject! History! Geography! Theory, grammar, semantics, pathology, mathematics, biology, anatomy, pedagogy, astronomy, hydrography, geology, psychiatry, religion, calisthenics, mineralogy, linguistics, statistics, geometry! [*Like mad, about to burst*] SCIENCE! All science! Everything! Chiromancy, phrenology, chiropractic, surgery! Techno ... [*Miss Margarida collapses in the word "technology"; she has a stroke. The scene must be serious and strongly dramatic. She drags herself on the floor and cries pathetically for help. The bell rings announcing the end of the second class.*] Help! Help me! [*She faints. The same student of the preceding times goes on-*

stage, more awkward than ever. He feels sorry for Miss Margarida and gives her a fantastic massage on her chest. This massage could have something erotic in it. Slowly, Miss Margarida seems to recuperate. As she gets better, the student stops the massage and becomes progressively afraid of her. Finally Miss Margarida gets up. The student withdraws in fear, always staring at Miss Margarida's movements, and then, at a reasonable distance, he stops as if petrified. Miss Margarida resumes her usual composure, looks around, and finally speaks in a new tone not yet used in the play. It should be sincere, pathetic, and terrible.] I am sorry. Miss Margarida shouldn't get excited. It isn't the first time Miss Margarida has had that. It was a theory attack in the coronary vein. Miss Margarida has a condition and she should be very careful. Miss Margarida promises it will never happen again. You must not worry, because Miss Margarida is *not* going to die. Miss Margarida will always be with you. Miss Margarida will never stop teaching you. Today it's you. Tomorrow it will be your children. And afterward the children of your children. Miss Margarida *always* will be here. Generation after generation. Miss Margarida is not perfect. We all have our shortcomings, don't we? You have to accept Miss Margarida the way she is. Miss Margarida will be *always* like this. And Miss Margarida will never leave you. But the bell has already rung. Miss Margarida doesn't want to hold you any longer. Miss Margarida wants you all to go home and think a lot about what you have learned today. In these two classes of Miss Margarida's. Miss Margarida also wants you to rest. You cannot live by work alone. Miss Margarida wants all of you here for the next lesson. Miss Margarida has still many things to teach you. Now go to your homes and to your families. And remember the words of Miss Margarida: always do what is good. That's the only way to happiness. Do always what is good. Good-bye. [*With those words, said absolutely without irony, Miss Margarida exits. On the stage, freed of her magnetic presence, two things should call attention: (1) The student, petrified, staring at the void. (2) Miss Margarida's* handbag, *large and out of fashion, which was forgotten on the table. Finding himself alone, the student relaxes and looks about the stage. Eventually he concentrates on the forgotten handbag. Curiosity wins: he opens the bag and takes out a colorful piece of candy. Then, in a crescendo, he takes out more and more candy of all shapes and colors (chocolate bars, lollipops, chewing gum, whatnot). He then gets to the bottom and takes out a large and frightening* gun. *Understanding nothing of what he sees, the student places the gun on the table already covered with sweets. He hesitates, clearly afraid that Miss Margarida might reappear. Hesitatingly he chooses a piece of candy. Opens it, bites it, doesn't like it, spits it out, chooses another piece, opens it, bites it, likes it, swallows it. Starts feeling guilty. Hesitates about opening a third piece of candy. Withdraws from table. Without taking a third piece of candy, the student goes back to his desk.]*

END